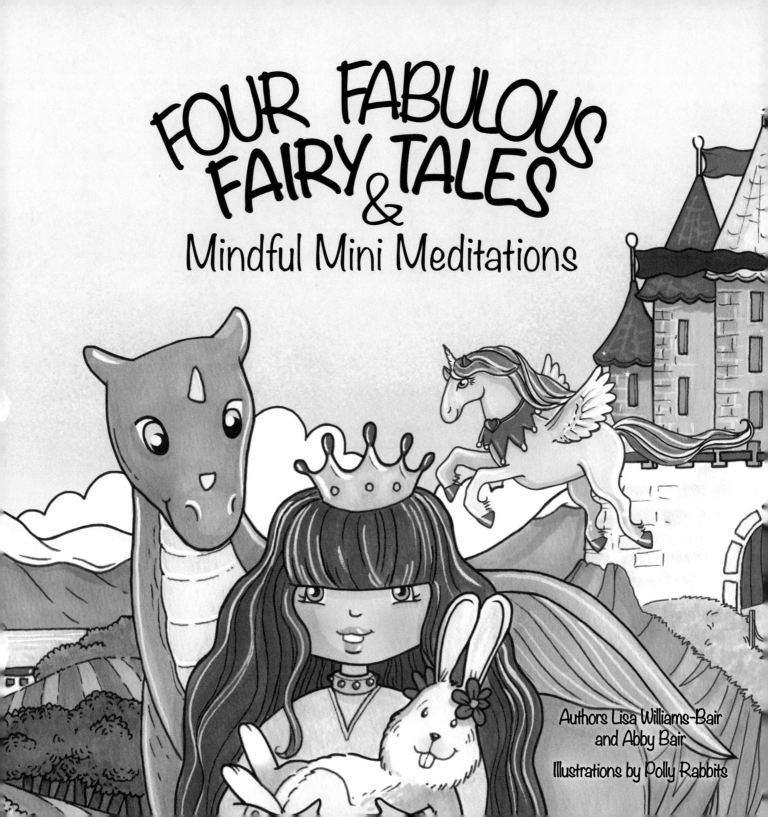

FOUR FABULOUS FAIRY & TALES

Mindful Mini Meditations

Authors Lisa Williams-Bair
and Abby Bair

Illustrations by Polly Rabbits

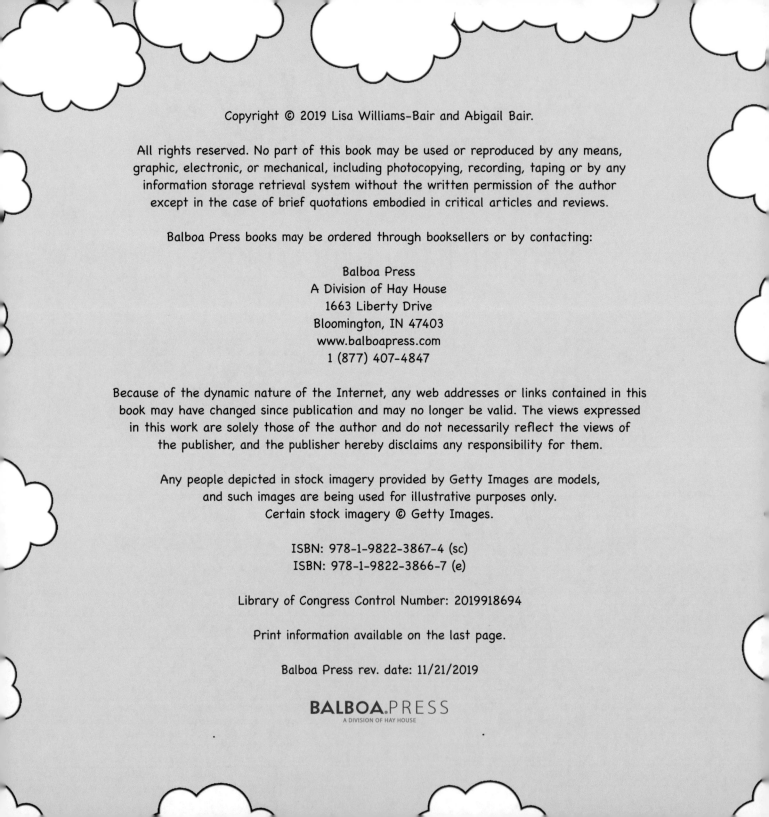

Balboa Press books may be ordered through booksellers or by contacting:

Balboa Press
A Division of Hay House
1663 Liberty Drive
Bloomington, IN 47403
www.balboapress.com
1 (877) 407-4847

ISBN: 978-1-9822-3867-4 (sc)
ISBN: 978-1-9822-3866-7 (e)

Library of Congress Control Number: 2019918694

Print information available on the last page.

Balboa Press rev. date: 11/21/2019

BALBOA.PRESS
A DIVISION OF HAY HOUSE

DEDICATION

TO MY ABIGAIL:

YOU ARE MY MIRACLE

MY HEART IS FULL.

You Complete Me.

Thank you.

ACKNOWLEDGEMENT

I WANT TO THANK YOU MY DEAR SISTER MERRY FOR YOUR ENCOURAGEMENT AND BRIANSTORMING IDEAS THAT HELPED TAKE THIS BOOK FROM A DREAM TO A REALITY.

THANKS TO MY SOUL SISTER C. KAY UHLES FOR YOUR EXCELLENT WRITING, EDITING/ SKILLS, ALSO NANCY SAUCEDA FOR SPIRITAL INPUT FOR THIS BOOK.

AND SHARI SCHWARZ FOR HER PROFESSIONAL EDITING AND OPTIMISM WITH HEART AS WELL.

Contents

Abigail's Self-Love Story

Once upon a time, there was a beautiful, young princess named Abigail, with long, flowing honey-brown hair. "Abby Bair" was her nickname. She lived in a magnificent purple castle in the forest.

She lived there with her mother, the caring Queen and her father, the helpful King. She was an only child and had wished for a sibling to play with, but instead she was walking out behind the castle by the stables and discovered a four- legged playmate.

It was a special friend named Buttercup, her most favorite horse in the Kingdom. He had a handsome mane, the color of her hair—honey-brown. His coat was soft and shiny. He was not a tall horse, but the perfect size for the princess to hop on and ride. Abby Bair cherished riding him every day.

They would take long rides into the meadow behind the pretty purple castle. The meadow was colorful with rolling green hills.

Princess "Abby Bair" could see big yellow daisies and bright red tulips sprinkled in the meadow with the vibrant green rolling hills. Can you see it? If you close your eyes, you can use your imagination. What do you see?

They traveled thru the meadow, near a pond with crystal clear, sparkling water that Buttercup could take a refreshing drink from. While Abby Bair waited for Buttercup, she slid off his back and gazed into the crystal, clear pond.

What do you think she saw in the pond?

She saw a glorious reflection of her lovely face! She smiled at her reflection and said, "I love you!" Her reflection said, "You know, Abby Bair, there are many pieces of yourself to love: Happy girl, sad girl, funny girl, sleepy girl, mad girl, quiet girl, leader, follower—these are just a few and I love them all!"

Can you close your eyes and see these pieces of you?

As you fill your heart with love for yourself, you can love and embrace (hug) all the parts of you. As you tell yourself this, each part of you feels loved and accepted.

You will set yourself free to be you! Peaceful, happy, content—that is your true self.

Abby Bair's reflection said, "Thank you for discovering the true you!"

Then Abby Bair and Buttercup rode off into the warm sunset and were back home in time for dinner. It was a good day.

The End.

Abigail's Self-Love Meditation

As you sit quietly in your room or find somewhere comfortable with pillows or a blanket around you, take a deep breath in, and then blow it out gently.

Close your eyes, and go within so you can connect with yourself and quiet your mind.

Listen to your breath. Breathe in slowly. Let your tummy fill up with air. Let your breath out gently.

When you focus on your breath, you can let the other thoughts from this day flow out of your body with your out breaths.

Do this, five times. Relax. Just be here, now. Once you feel calm and peaceful, you are ready.

Allow your imagination to come out and play with you!

It is time to picture in your mind, a princess or a prince. She or he is you.

You are riding your horse into a meadow with rolling green hills and colorful flowers. Can you see it?

Can you smell the fresh grass, flowers and clean air?

Breathe in slowly. See it. Feel it. Then breathe out in a serene way.

What does your meadow look like?

You can share it out loud or just see it in your mind.

Can you picture this lovely meadow with all its beauty? Then as you hop off your horse, see yourself walking up to a pond. This pond has crystal-clear, sparkling, water.

While you wait for your horse to take a refreshing drink, you look down into the crystal-clear water. What do you see?

You see yourself! A beautiful face in the water. It is your reflection. Your reflection is *full of love for you.*

Your reflection says to you the Prince or Princess, *"I love you! I love all of you!"*

There are many pieces of yourself to love. There are many sides to you.

There are parts like happy self, sad self, funny self, mad self, quiet self, loud self, leader or follower self.

What other parts of yourself do you see or feel? Share if you want

We are made of the most amazing stuff! Love and embrace all of you. Give yourself a big hug!

Ah... isn't that nice! As you fill your heart with love and acceptance of all of you, it will set you free to be you!

Your reflection says, "Thank you, self. You have discovered the real, true you!"

As you climb back on your horse, you ride off into the warm sunset and back home for dinner. It was a good day.

Then you sit in your comfy spot, be thankful for this time you spent connecting to your inside self. Share it with someone, if you like, or write it down in a special journal where you can write out your thoughts and feelings.

Blessings and so it is.

Kiki's Unconditional Love

Once upon a time, there was a cheerful rosy-colored unicorn named Kiki. She was the leader of the unicorns in her village. This unicorn lived in a magical country-side with cute little barns that were houses for her and her unicorn friends. Kiki's rosy pink coat had a special meaning to it. It meant that she was **unconditionally loving** to herself and to all the other unicorns in her village.

No matter what, she accepted herself and the others just as they were.

She would shine her cheerful rosiness down upon her friends, *blessing them* when she flew by.

Kiki went to visit her best friend named Pucca. Pucca was the princess in their village. She was a gentle lavender which represented **peace..**

The two unicorns had a special job, as the leaders in the village, to *bless the world,* sharing their colors from within.

They would soar through the air, spreading *unconditional love and peace* throughout the land.

Leaders Kiki and Princess Pucca, each had a special glow they would shine, for it was a light from within them which they were born with. This special shiny glow had powers to help each unicorn in the village understand that THIS *unconditional love, and peace was inside them too!*

One day as they glided above the village, they looked down and saw little Skylar, a unicorn sitting in the middle of a meadow. He looked sad.

Kiki and Pucca stopped. "Why are you sad?"

"I am not connected to my color inside," Skylar said. "I feel separate and alone."

"Your coat of fur is the color sky-blue," Kiki explained. "It represents the sky and sea which symbolize harmony."

Skylar asked, "What is harmony and how can I feel harmony inside myself? I want to feel it and share it with others just like you do!"

"Harmony is a calmness inside you," Kiki said. "It is when you and everyone around you are getting along and feeling happy."

"Wow!" he said. "If I was born with it, it must be in there!"

"Yes, it is," they said.

Skylar closed his eyes, took five deep breaths, and began to feel calm and harmonious inside.

Princess Pucca said, "When you feel good inside, it's a sign that you are connected to that special gift you were born with!"

Little Skylar smiled and thanked the two special unicorns. His sky-blue color glowed warmly all around him and the others.

"Yes! I see it and I feel it coming from you Little Skylar!" said Kiki. "Now you are connecting with it from within you!"

They all flew together throughout the land, sharing their gifts and helping others realize they have these qualities inside them too!

What is your gift? Do you know? It is within you.

Feel the energy of love in your heart and the message of your gift will come to you.

Once you feel it inside, you can share it with others. I invite you to try it today!

The End

KIKI'S Unconditional Love Meditation

As you sit quietly in your room or find somewhere comfortable with pillows or a blanket around you, take a deep breath in, and then blow it out gently.

Close your eyes, and go within so you can connect with yourself and quiet your mind.

Listen to your breath. Breathe in slowly. Let your tummy fill up with air. Let your breath out gently.

When you focus on your breath, you can let the other thoughts from this day flow out of your body with your **out** breaths.

Do this, five times. Relax. Just be here, now. Once you feel calm and peaceful, you are ready.

Close your eyes for just a few minutes and imagine these beautiful unicorns. Can you see their colors of rosy pink, lavender and sky blue?

Notice them flying through the village, blessing everyone as they go. See leader Kiki with her shiny, rosy coat of pink, loving herself, and shining that loving energy down to everyone no matter what they do or say!

Do you feel love in your heart? What does it feel like or look like?

Can you picture her friend Princess Pucca, soaring in the air with a soft lavender glow flowing out of her? She floats into the village, sending peace to all.

Do you feel peace inside your mind or body? What does it feel like or look like?

Then, here comes Skylar, around the corner. He is smiling and gliding thru the village, feeling happy and bringing harmony to everyone there!

Breathe in and blow the air out gently. As you relax, try to feel these qualities inside your mind and body.

Are you harmonious and happy? Do you feel content inside your mind and body?

What does it feel like to you?

As you sit in your comfy spot, be thankful for this time you spent connecting to your inside self. Share it with someone, if you like, or write it down in a special journal where you can write out your thoughts and feelings.

In your mind, see the beauty of these colors within you and discover what color your gift is. Then you can share it with those around you and with the world!

Blessings to you.

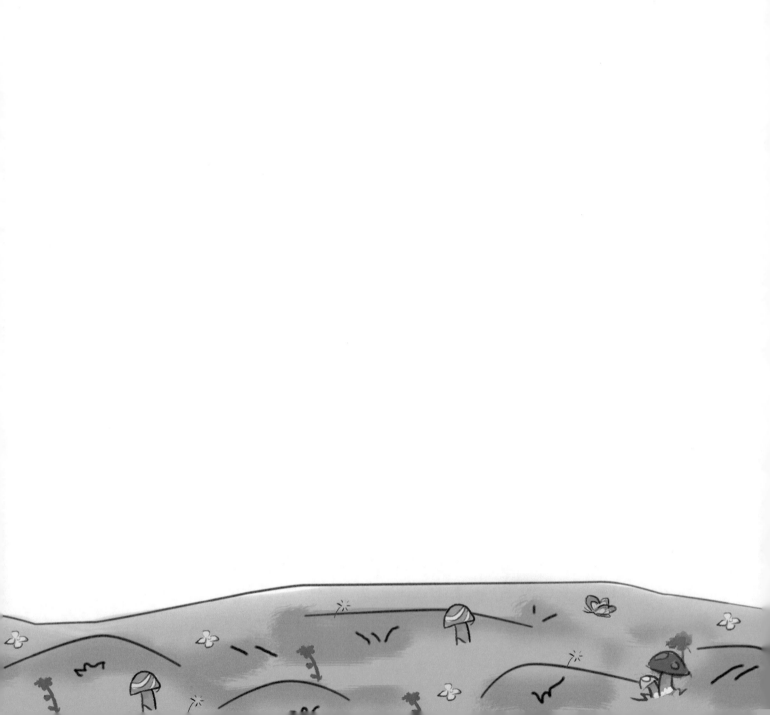

The Shy Princess, Ferret and the Fairies

Once upon a time, there was a shimmering pink castle high up on a hill. It overlooked a kingdom full of happy people ruled by a king and queen who were kind and wise.

There was a sweet and compassionate royal highness, Chloe, who also lived there. She had long, cascading chestnut brown hair, with gentle green eyes, and a smile bright enough to light up the kingdom!

31

Chloe had a pet bunny named Clover. The friendly bunny had soft white fur, pink perky ears, and a rosy nose that wiggled with glee! She was her only friend. Chloe was shy and had a hard time talking to people. She wished that she was more confident and had the courage to talk to people in the village.

Princess Chloe and Clover the bunny went for a ride on her princess bicycle. They were looking for a fun activity in the village. Ready for an adventure, Clover hopped into the white basket on the handlebars.

The two friends traveled to many places on their bicycle, but today was an unusual day. They rode down the bumpy hill that the shimmering pink castle sat on and took a turn into the village full of festive folks.

As they rode through the kingdom, waving at the people, they came upon a boy who was smiling and holding a fuzzy grey ferret with mischievous eyes and a sweet face. The ferret had a secret to share and he wanted the princess to come to visit the forest nearby.

He jumped out of the boy's hands and scampered into the magical forest with Chloe and Clover not far behind.

The forest was full of whimsical creatures and fast flying fairies who were friends with the ferret. They were happy to see him scutter into the forest. The ferret knew that the fairies were blessed with special glimmering gold fairy dust. (That was his secret.)

The fairies saw Princess Chloe coming into the forest. One flew to her and whispered in her ear, "You have a power inside you, Princess Chloe, and you can create whatever you want in your life!

Close your eyes and use your imagination to see what you want. Be in your mind or feel it in your heart. Let me sprinkle this shimmery dust on your head. It will come to you in magical ways."

The ferret said, "Trust and receive your good now! Listen to your inner voice and take action. You can use your outer voice to talk to others and make friends!"

The empowering message from the fairies meant Princess Chloe would feel stronger inside and more confident. Princess Chloe and her bunny Clover were inspired by this information. With their mind, heart, and soul, enjoyed the good feelings and creative thoughts they had about being confident.

Now, she would go up to someone and introduce herself. She felt self-assured this was possible now!

They rode back into the village and Chloe saw a group of girls she wanted to meet. She hopped off her bike and slowly walked over to them. Clover was saying go!

Chloe nervously nodded and said, "Hello, my name is Princess Chloe. Can I play hopscotch with you?"
The girls said, "Sure, we would love to play with you!"

41

Princess Chloe discovered this power of being confident, was something she had all along! She realized she could be sure of herself and not shy anymore.

You have this power to create what you want in your life too!

How would you use this power to be more confident about doing something you desire in your life?

With this knowledge you can live happily ever after, like the princess, fairies and the ferret did.

Shy Princess, Ferret and the Fairies Meditation

As you sit quietly in your room or find somewhere comfortable with pillows or a blanket around you, take a deep breath in and blow it out gently.

Do this, five times. Close your eyes for just a few minutes and imagine yourself riding your bike down through the village, where all the happy people live.

You follow the ferret into the magical forest where the fairies are.

As you look around, there are lush green trees and moss on the ground, the sun is peeking through, shining down on you.

Do you feel the warm sunshine's rays upon you?

What does it feel like or look like to you?

Then, you walk down a little bit on the path, you see these beautiful fairies. See them flitting around you with shimmering gold fairy dust, floating down on you.

"Hello little fairies what are you doing here today?" you ask.

The fairies say hello in return and they begin to whisper to you about the power that you have inside you to create anything you want in your life.

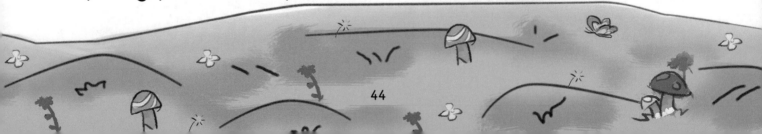

This is something you may not have known about yourself. You have had it inside all along, since you were born!

Your dreams can come true if you follow your heart and open your mind. You can discover ideas in your mind, heart and soul.

Can you take a moment to feel in your heart, and listen to what it wants?

You may realize you could create new friends, confidence, and an attitude of cheerful thoughts and actions.

Wow! What an empowering message from the fairies. This means that now you can and will feel stronger inside and more confident!

You can practice this with your mind, heart, and soul and enjoy the good feelings and creative thoughts you have.

How would you use this power and what good could you create in your life?

With this knowledge you can live happily ever after, like the fairies, ferret, and the princess did.

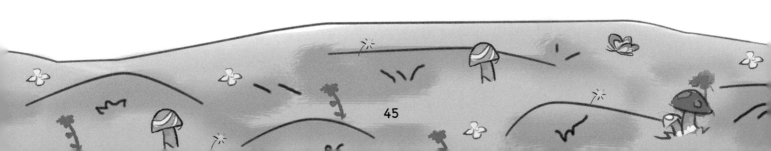

The Kind Twins and the Dapper Dragon

Once upon a time, there was a little prince named Albert and he had a twin sister, Princess Alice, who was very kind. They both had sandy blonde hair, fair-skin and brilliant blue eyes. The twins would spend many hours frolicking up and down the hallways of an impressive grey stone castle on a hill.

One day Albert and Alice were skipping down a long hallway, and they saw a big brown wooden door they had not noticed before.

The young prince was adventurous, and he wanted to open the door to the unknown, so he asked his sister, "Shall I open it?"

She was the cautious one of the two and replied, "Do you think it's safe?"

Prince Albert said, "I'm not sure, but let's check it out!" He wanted to discover something new. He slowly opened the door and they both peeked their heads in.

They saw an enchanted meadow with little fairies flitting in the air and dapper green dragons walking around.

The little prince noticed a big ol' dapper dragon with dark green spots, sleeping by a tree. Prince Albert wanted to be friends with the dragon, to play with him and go for a ride.

The prince thought, *If I send him a kind message thru my mind, the spotted dragon might understand.*

So, he focused with his good energy and thought, *I want to be your friend. I will not hurt you.* As he set this intention to befriend the dragon, the children carefully walked up to it and Albert actually touched the soft, fuzzy fur on the dragon. Then he began to climb up on this dragon.

Alice said, "Oh my! Are you sure about that?"

He said, "Yes, I sent the dragon a message and put some good energy toward him, so it knows I like him!"

As he sat there on the spotted green dragon's back, he imagined surrounding the dragon with love and light. The dragon gradually began to open his sleepy emerald green eyes.

Prince Albert smiled down at him and Princess Alice stood there frozen, unsure of what was to come.

The little prince said, "I would like to be your friend. Do you want to be my friend?"

The dragon said, "Yes, I will be your friend, but I do not know how. Can you show me?"

Princess Alice wasn't afraid anymore. She talked with the dragon about how friends treat each other, such as be kind, say nice things to one another, and share your toys.

The dragon got an idea of how to be kind! He said to Alice, "I like your teeth!"

Thank you, the little princess said, I like your cool dragon tail!"

The dragon said, "What a nice thing to say!" The dragon smiled at her.

They all played together and enjoyed each other's company as new friends.

If you are kind and friendly, act with good thoughts and actions. You can create a kind and loving world to live in!

The End

The Kind Twins and Dapper Dragon Mediation

As you sit quietly in your room or find somewhere comfortable with pillows or a blanket around you, take a deep breath in, and then blow it out gently.

Close your eyes, and go within so you can connect with yourself and quiet your mind.

Listen to your breath. Breathe in slowly. Let your tummy fill up with air. Let your breath out gently.

When you focus on your breath, you can let the other thoughts from this day flow out of your body with your out breaths.

Do this, five times. Relax. Just be here, now. Once you feel calm and peaceful, you are ready.

Close your eyes for just a few minutes and imagine a beautiful big grey stone castle on a hill. Do you see the Prince and Princess inside in a hallway frolicking, and playing with a ball. Can you picture yourself in there too?

What does it look like, feel like to you, in that grand castle with the Royals?

Fun yes!

An adventure is about to unfold in your mind as all three of you, walk down the hallway, to the big brown door and open it, what do you see? Prince and Princess see a beautiful meadow……

Can you see the rolling green hills and smell the sweet - scented flowers? Can you imagine the cute little fairies flitting around you, they are happy you are here.

Then behind the tree, a mighty sight, a Dapper Dragon with big dark green spots, sleeping peacefully. You and the Royals decide to walk closer to this dragon.

The little Princess wanted so much, to be friends with this dragon, she wanted to ask him to play with them. After sending loving energy to the Dapper Dragon, you decided to reach up and pet the dragon's soft velvet nose! Then you watch the little adventurous Prince climb up on him!

As that dragon opens his sleepy emerald eyes, he sees you and you see him!

You, the Prince and Princess show the dragon kindness. You are not afraid for you know in your heart he is a good - natured dragon.

You and the Dapper Dragon have a wonderful time being kind to each other, with the Prince and Princess, saying delightful things to one another.

Can you imagine sending someone love and walking towards them to say something nice? Give it a try, being kind, giving love and open your heart will do the trick!

You can then receive love and kindness, It can come from another person or a *dragon* and you can *change* the world into a kind world to live in!

As you sit in your comfy spot, be thankful for this time you spent connecting to your inside self. Share it with someone, if you like, or write it down in a special journal where you can write out your thoughts and feelings.

The end.

Lisa Williams-Bair, RScF, thrives on inspiring and empowering children, teens and adults, reminding each student of the beauty and gifts within themselves and others! Over the last 25 years, Lisa has taught various methods of meditation, leading people to experience the life they desire. Lisa knows the benefits of meditation and was moved when she felt the calling to co-create Four Fabulous Fairy Tales and Mindful Mini Meditations with her daughter, Abby.

Abigail, "Abby," has blessed the world with her kind heart, beautiful smile, and inspiring talents. She enjoys performing in talent shows, playing soccer, walking her dog, Lucy, and snuggling with her kitties, Sugar and Sir Blue. Abby flourishes when she interacts with small children and when she writes children's stories that speak to the heart, mind and soul of children and parents alike.

Printed in the United States
By Bookmasters